AMAZING HOCKEY STORIES

HAYLEY WICKENHEISER

Lorna Schultz Nicholson

Illustrations by D. A. Bishop

Scholastic Canada Ltd.
Toronto New York London Auckland Sydney
Mexico City New Delhi Hong Kong Buenos Aires

With huge thanks to Hayley for all she has done to empower
girls and women. You are a true role model. — *L. S. N.*

Scholastic Canada Ltd.
604 King Street West, Toronto, Ontario M5V 1E1, Canada

Scholastic Inc.
557 Broadway, New York, NY 10012, USA

Scholastic Australia Pty Limited
PO Box 579, Gosford, NSW 2250, Australia

Scholastic New Zealand Limited
Private Bag 94407, Botany, Manukau 2163, New Zealand

Scholastic Children's Books
Euston House, 24 Eversholt Street, London NW1 1DB, UK

www.scholastic.ca

Library and Archives Canada Cataloguing in Publication
Schultz Nicholson, Lorna, author
Hayley Wickenheiser / Lorna Schultz Nicholson ; illustrated by D.A. Bishop.

(Amazing hockey stories)
ISBN 978-1-4431-6309-5 (softcover)

1. Wickenheiser, Hayley, 1978- --Juvenile literature. 2. Women hockey
players--Canada--Biography--Juvenile literature. I. Bishop, D. A., author
II. Title. III. Series: Schultz Nicholson, Lorna. Amazing hockey stories.

GV848.5.W52S38 2018   j796.962092   C2018-900093-7

Photos ©: cover: Bruce Bennett/Getty Images; cover background: Nik Merkulov/
Shutterstock; 5: Andrew Francis Wallace/Toronto Star/Getty Images; 11: Hockey
Canada Images; 28: Lutz Bongarts/Getty Images; 35: Bernard Weil/Toronto Star/Getty
Images; 37: Peter Power/Toronto Star/Getty Images; 50: Brian Bahr/Getty Images; 54:
Christopher Morris/Corbis/Getty Images; 62: Courtesy of Hayley Wickenheiser and
Dave Holland; 64: Mikki Adams.

All other photos courtesy of Hayley Wickenheiser.

Text copyright © 2018 by Lorna Shultz Nicholson
Illustrations copyright © 2018 by Scholastic Canada Ltd.
All rights reserved.

6 5 4 3 2 1   Printed in Malaysia 108   18 19 20 21 22

CONTENTS

BEST IN THE WORLD

After playing on the Canadian National Team for 23 years, Hayley Wickenheiser decided it was time to hang up her skates. On January 14, 2017, in a ceremony held at the brand new Rogers Place in Edmonton just before the Oilers were to play the Calgary Flames, Hayley spoke to the crowd of over 18,000. Although she had played 276 games for Team Canada and earned 379 points in those games (including 168 goals), had won multiple MVP trophies, five Olympic medals and six World Championship gold medals, was named to the Order of Canada and had an arena named after her, she feels her biggest accomplishment was making girls feel accepted in hockey arenas. Hayley is proud that girls can "walk into a hockey rink with a bag and stick and feel welcome."

Hayley's retirement ceremony was the first of its kind. Usually women's hockey and the NHL aren't combined, but her groundbreaking career made it fitting. With her fierce determination, competitive spirit and outspoken attitude, she proved to the hockey world that girls could play at a high level. Hockey legend Wayne Gretzky addressed Hayley directly that night, saying, "You've touched so many lives. You've opened so many doors for so many young girls to be able one day to win a gold medal." Then he said, "You're the female Gordie Howe."

Hayley's entrance into hockey wasn't always easy. Many people didn't accept that a girl could skate and shoot, pass and make great plays, sometimes better than the boys. Over the years she changed that attitude. Go, Hayley, go!

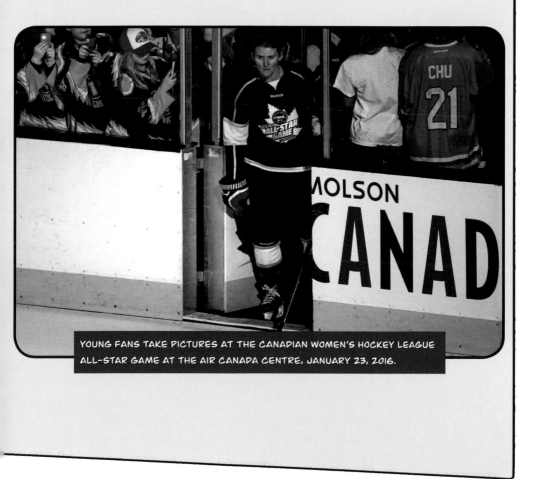

YOUNG FANS TAKE PICTURES AT THE CANADIAN WOMEN'S HOCKEY LEAGUE ALL-STAR GAME AT THE AIR CANADA CENTRE, JANUARY 23, 2016.

EARLY DAYS

HAYLEY, WITH ROOM TO GROW IN HER HOCKEY PANTS, LOOKS READY FOR ACTION IN HER FIRST HOCKEY CARD PHOTO.

Hayley Wickenheiser laced up her first pair of skates in Shaunavon, Saskatchewan, where the flat prairie landscape and cold winter temperatures are perfect for outdoor skating and shinny. She learned how to skate on a backyard rink that her father made. He used two-by-fours to build the frame and spent hours watering the rink with a garden hose to make perfect ice. The neighbourhood kids were always over playing pickup hockey, and six-year-old Hayley loved to join in, playing until her toes were frozen. Hockey was a family affair, and Hayley's family knew a little something about hockey because her cousin, Doug Wickenheiser, played in the NHL.

A GIRL ON THE BOYS' TEAM

In 1985, when Hayley was seven, she wanted to play minor hockey like her neighbourhood friends. But Shaunavon's population was only 2,100, so there weren't many minor teams and not a single one for girls. Back in the 1980s, women's hockey wasn't a very popular sport in the Prairies. In fact it was almost non-existent, especially in small towns. All Hayley knew was that she wanted to play hockey. And if she had to join a boys' team, that's what she would do. So she did.

No one really expected much from "the girl," but it was quickly apparent that Hayley had a keen hockey sense. She could skate and shoot, and often played better than the boys on her team. She had natural talent, but she also practised her shots, crossovers and backwards skating all the time on her backyard rink. Once her father woke up in the middle of the night to find Hayley outside, shooting pucks in the dark! The extra work was helping her develop a hard shot and superior skating skills.

NINE-YEAR-OLD HAYLEY PLAYS BACKYARD HOCKEY WITH HER SEVEN-YEAR-OLD BROTHER ROSS IN SHAUNAVON, SASKATCHEWAN.

Each fall when it was time to sign up for hockey, Hayley's parents asked her if she still wanted to join a boys' team. She always said yes. Hayley loved playing hockey even if she was the only girl. The boys on her team accepted Hayley and liked playing with her —

she helped them win! But not everyone was happy that Hayley was playing hockey with the boys.

When Hayley was nine, she wanted to attend a summer hockey camp in Swift Current, but the organizers told her mother that she wasn't allowed to register because she was a girl. Her mother thought that was unfair and fought for Hayley's right to play. She threatened to go to Saskatchewan's Human Rights Commission with the case. The camp begrudgingly gave Hayley permission to attend after all. But at the end of the session one of the organizers told her, "You'll never be a hockey player, Hayley." She was so mad . . . and was going to prove him wrong.

When Hayley first started playing on boys' teams, there were no change rooms for girls. She had to put her gear on at home and walk to the arena already dressed. People thought she would quit. But she didn't. And each time her team travelled to another city, they had to figure out where Hayley could change. If she was lucky, she was allowed to dress in the referees' room. Most of the time she had to change in public washrooms, which was embarrassing. Girls would come in and laugh at her, and mothers of the boys she played against would make mean comments. Once, when the women's restroom was being renovated,

Hayley had to change in a small, makeshift plywood room, out in the arena's front lobby, where everyone was coming in and out. She was mortified.

Because Hayley had to change separately from her teammates, she often had to walk alone, past all the other parents, to get to the ice. She tried tucking her hair under her helmet, but many of them still knew she was a girl. Sometimes they would tell her that she shouldn't be playing hockey — some of them didn't like Hayley playing because she was better than their sons.

A TEAM OF HER OWN

In March of 1990, when Hayley was 11, she had a huge, wonderful shock. She saw an all-female hockey team play for the first time — on TV! The first-ever IIHF Women's World Championship was being played in Ottawa, Ontario, and televised all across Canada. The Team Canada players wore pink jerseys and white pants, and they skated like pros. They deked the goalie and shot the puck in the top corners. It was hockey like Hayley had never seen before. She was glued to the TV for every game the Canadian women played.

Before this game, Hayley's heroes had been Wayne Gretzky and Mark Messier. Suddenly, she had new ones: France St-Louis and Geraldine Heaney! When Canada won the gold medal in a crazy fast game against the United States, Hayley decided that one day she was going to play on an all-girls team and win a gold medal, too.

SUSIE YUEN CELEBRATES WINNING GOLD IN THE 1990 IIHF WOMEN'S WORLD CHAMPIONSHIP IN OTTAWA, ONTARIO.

HAYLEY, AGE 12, SUITED UP FOR THE BLACKFOOT COUGARS.

During the summer that Hayley turned 12, she and her family moved to Calgary, Alberta. Hayley would be going into second-year peewee hockey, and the boys were getting bigger every year. But Calgary was a big city and there were enough girls playing that there were girls' teams. So for the first time, Hayley tried out for a girls' team, the Blackfoot Cougars — and easily made it. At first it was strange for Hayley to be playing with other girls. She was finally allowed to be in a dressing room with her teammates, and she liked being able to dress, talk and joke around with the girls. But there were a few things she had to get used to. If boys had a disagreement, it sometimes got physical, but then they would be back to being friends right away. Not the girls. Now a tiff sometimes lasted for weeks! And sometimes she missed the hard shots and more physical game the boys played.

While playing with the Cougars that season, Hayley found out that women's hockey would be included in the 1991 Canada Games for the first time ever — and that there was going to be a team from Alberta! The Canada Games would take place in Prince Edward Island from February 17 to March 2, and the team would be for ages 18 and under. Everyone thought that Hayley was too young to be on the team. Hockey at that level was very different than she had played before. The skill level was higher, especially the playmaking, and the players were much more mature. The stakes were suddenly much higher. But Hayley didn't care. She wanted to try out anyway.

THE CANADA GAMES

In February Hayley flew from Alberta to Prince Edward Island and proudly wore the Team Alberta jersey. She was the only 12-year-old on the team. Some of the other players were 17 and in high school. But Hayley got over her initial shyness of changing in front of all the older girls because it didn't matter. She was part of the team! And their team was doing well.

Team Alberta had made it to the gold medal final against Team British Columbia. When it was time for the game, Hayley was so excited. Her family were in the stands, waving handmade signs. But when Hayley stepped on the ice she didn't wave back — she knew she had to focus. Hayley skated fast and kept moving so she'd be in front of the net, ready to pick up a loose puck and take a shot. She got the opportunity she was looking for and blasted a shot on British Columbia's net. The puck flew over the goalie's left blocker. Hayley threw her arms in the air. She had scored what ended up being the winning goal!

After the game both teams lined up to get their medals. Hayley was proud to have the gold around her neck. Then she heard them announce her name. She had been named MVP for the gold medal game!

Hayley was all smiles as she went back to the

dressing room. But she was in for an unpleasant surprise. The team manager told her she had to do a test for performance-enhancing drugs. What? Hayley couldn't believe it — she was only 12! Game officials gave her a plastic bottle and told her to urinate into it. Shocked, Hayley went to the bathroom stall. She'd only ever done this at the doctor's office, when her mother was with her. She wished her mom was with her now — it was just so weird and gross.

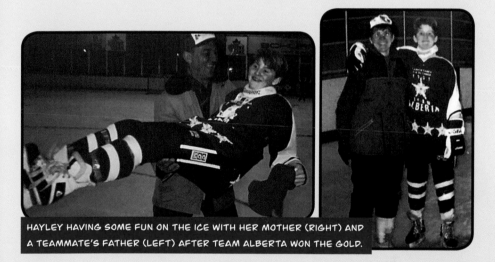

HAYLEY HAVING SOME FUN ON THE ICE WITH HER MOTHER (RIGHT) AND A TEAMMATE'S FATHER (LEFT) AFTER TEAM ALBERTA WON THE GOLD.

BACK WITH THE BOYS

After the Canada Games, Hayley finished a fabulous year with the peewee Blackfoot Cougars. They won the gold medal in their Girls Hockey Calgary division. But when it came time to enroll in her first year of bantam, she decided to try out for the AAA Bantam Bruins in the elite Northwest Calgary quadrant boys' hockey program. She wanted to learn new things and improve in a tougher, more physical game. Hayley stepped on the ice for evaluations knowing she had to shine because there were a lot of boys who really wanted to make this team. So she tucked her hair under her helmet and pretended she was one of them.

After grinding it out — and taking her fair share of hits — she made the team! But once the season started, some of the boys from the other teams were obviously out to bully her on the ice. Sometimes they held their sticks high to knock her helmet — hard. They made cheap shots and got many high-sticking calls. Hayley's own team had her back, though, and before every game her coach would tell her who to watch out for. But he couldn't help much with the parents who would hang over the glass and yell rude comments at her. Hayley learned to ignore them. There were bigger and better things to focus on.

In July of 1992, it was announced that, for the first time ever, women's hockey would be included in the Winter Olympics starting in Nagano, Japan, in 1998. Hayley jumped up and down. Women's hockey in the Olympics! Hayley had a new dream now . . . oh, how she wanted to make that Olympic Team! Hayley was still only 14 and there were only a few years to make that very big dream happen.

A SERIOUS SETBACK

When Hayley aged out of bantam, the next opportunity was the Northwest Calgary AAA midget team. This would not be an easy team to make. The boys trying out were now big teenagers. Competition was fierce — many of them would not make the cut. Hayley had added a perfected wrist shot to her repertoire. She skated hard, and made the team.

Then, ten games into the season, the team was returning from a tournament in Medicine Hat and Hayley was getting her bag from the bus. The coach told her he wanted to see her in his office. After he ushered her in, he told Hayley he was cutting her. She was shocked. She'd made the team. Why now? The coach admitted that he didn't know how to deal with having a girl on the team. He just couldn't handle the pressure.

Hayley left his office and went outside to find her mother. She got into the car and stared straight ahead. "I just got cut," she said. Her mother was stunned. Would they always have to fight for Hayley to play? They drove over to the coordinator's house to discuss it. Hayley sat in the car and watched her mother march up to the front door. She knocked and knocked until it finally opened. But he wouldn't change his mind and wouldn't even discuss it. Hayley got her release papers . . . but she didn't have a team.

Hayley was not going to give up. She joined a senior women's hockey team in Calgary. Once again, she adjusted to being inside the dressing room. But this time it was different. Many of the women on this team were grown-ups with full-time jobs, and they were very serious about hockey. Hayley was just a teen in high school. Hayley had watched some of these players on television — in their infamous pink and white uniforms — in the 1990 Women's World Championship. She admired them. Hayley was suddenly challenged on a whole different level. She matured quickly. She learned what professionalism, character and teamwork were all about. And while Hayley was playing with the women's team, she got a huge opportunity. She was asked to try out for the Canadian National Team. At the age of 15, Hayley was being scouted by Hockey Canada.

THE INTERNATIONAL STAGE

In January of 1994, Hayley made the Canadian Women's National Team. The IIHF Women's World Championship was being held in Lake Placid, New York, that April. She had just a short time to master a somewhat different game than she had been playing. There was no hitting and the play was really fast. Hayley had to work to keep up. Stick-checking is an important skill in women's hockey and Hayley found her opponents could steal the puck from her too easily. She quickly learned to use different skills to defend the puck.

Three months later, Hayley played in her first World Championship in Lake Placid. At 15, she was the youngest player on the team. Superstar France St-Louis was 20 years older than Hayley. Hayley's roommate for the tournament was Margot Page, who was 30 years old. Margot was a school teacher and would help Hayley with her math homework back at their hotel room. Hayley learned a lot on and off the ice. She skated in three of the five games and earned her first international point, for an assist. She also earned her first international gold medal, when the Canadians beat the US team in the final.

SOFTBALL SEASON

Every year after the hockey season ended, Hayley would put down her stick and pick up her glove. She'd played softball since she was little. Just like in hockey, she was one of the best players. Two months after competing in the Hockey World Championship, Hayley competed in the Canadian Softball Midget Nationals and was named the All-Canadian shortstop and top hitter. The following year Hayley made the Junior National Softball Team and played for Canada at the 1995 Softball World Championship in Illinois. Shortly after, Hayley found out that softball would be a sport in the 1996 Summer Olympics in Atlanta, USA. She had a lot to think about. Hayley's ultimate goal was competing at the Olympics. Would softball be her opportunity, or hockey?

Hayley loved hockey, but she also hoped to earn a scholarship to play softball in the National Collegiate Athletic Association, or NCAA. So she switched back and forth. In the winter, she'd get her hockey teammates to hit ground balls to her in the arena hallways. In the summer, she'd fit in hockey camps around her softball schedule if she could. It's exceedingly difficult to be at the top of one sport, much less two, but Hayley tried to stick with both.

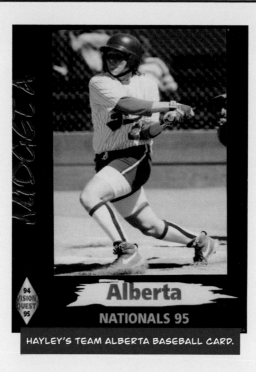

HAYLEY'S TEAM ALBERTA BASEBALL CARD.

THE ROAD TO NAGANO

The 1998 Olympic Winter Games and the debut of women's hockey as an Olympic sport were around the corner. Hayley had her eye firmly on her Olympic dream and decided to concentrate on hockey — she was determined to be on Team Canada. Hayley showed up to the camp in top physical condition. From her experience playing on the boys' teams Hayley knew how to protect the puck and shoot hard. Playing on the women's teams had honed her playmaking skills. Hayley made the cut! She would be on the first-ever Canadian women's Olympic hockey team.

As with other Olympic sports, a qualifying tournament decided which countries would compete in women's hockey at the Olympics. Spots would be based on the results of the 1997 IIHF Women's World Championship, to be held in Kitchener, Ontario. In Kitchener, Hayley stepped on the ice to fans cheering "Go, Canada, Go!" It was deafening. The team had never played in front of such a loud, rambunctious crowd. The place was jammed with fans wearing red and white and waving Canadian flags. And the Canadian team didn't disappoint, easily winning their round-robin games. But the final wouldn't be so easy. It was against their number one rival, the United States.

On April 6, 1997, Canada and the United States battled it out, giving more than 6,000 fans a show to remember. The game was like a ping-pong match, with goals going back and forth. Nancy Drolet scored for Canada at the end of the first period, but Team USA came back in the second. Then Canada scored again . . . and then so did the US. After the second period, the players went to the dressing room with a 2–2 tie. Hayley soaked in the energy of the building. The fans in Kitchener were going crazy out there! In the third period, Canada scored to take the lead but the US fought back and tied it up again. The game was going to overtime! The fans screamed and yelled "Go, Canada, Go!"

Fifteen tense minutes into overtime, Nancy Drolet scored her third goal for Canada. It was a big moment. Hayley threw her gloves in the air. The crowd was going crazy, and everyone was hugging. Canada had won the gold medal and qualified for the 1998 Olympics. Hayley's dream was alive.

THE 1998 WINTER OLYMPICS

The Olympics took place in Nagano, Japan, the following February. Hayley boarded the plane, proudly wearing her red and white Team Canada track suit. Canada's first women's hockey game took place on February 8, against Japan. Hayley assisted on the first and fifth goals and then scored the ninth. Canada won the game 13–0. It was a nice way to start. Canada's next game was against China. Canada won 2–0, with an assist by Hayley on the first goal of the game. The Canadian team went on to beat Sweden 5–3 and Finland 4–2. Canada was heading into their last round-robin game on a winning streak.

HAYLEY MAKES A PLAY IN THE 1998 OLYMPICS.

They were set to play their big rival, the United States. The Canadians had defeated them in Kitchener and weren't panicking — they knew they could win again. The game started off fast and furious, with both teams racing up and down the ice. Canada scored the first goal but their lead didn't last long — the US rallied to score. The first period ended with a 1–1 tie. Both teams had lots of opportunities in the second period, but neither was able to score. Back in their dressing room, the Canadians regrouped and discussed their game. The third period started with a blast. Canada came out strong and scored three fast goals to take a 4–1 lead.

But then something shocking happened: the United States scored six straight goals and won the game 7–4. After the game, the Canadian women discussed the loss. It wasn't great, but it wasn't the end of the world. The gold medal game was the one that counted, and Canada was set to face the US again for that. Hayley was positive that her team would win the coveted gold. They knew all of Canada would be cheering for them — they wanted that Olympic gold, too.

WHAT ARE HAYLEY'S NICKNAMES?

WICK, CHICKEN AND CHICKENHEISER!

YOU'RE INVITED

Although Canada did not win the gold, Hayley had played well. She had two goals and six assists in just six games. More people had started to notice her talent and how tough she was. So tough that Bobby Clarke, the general manager of the Philadelphia Flyers, invited Hayley to participate in the Flyers rookie camp that season. This time they made sure she had a dressing room. Gone were the days of changing in a public washroom or a lobby.

Bobby Clarke took Hayley under his wing and introduced her to the guys. Each day of camp had two tough dryland training sessions and an ice session. When the day was over, Hayley went back to her hotel room exhausted and collapsed into bed. The camp was incredibly tough but Hayley kept up. The Flyers were so impressed with her talent, drive and toughness that she was invited back for the 1999 session.

DRIVE FOR A DREAM

Even though Hayley had gone to the Olympics and trained all winter long for hockey, she still liked playing softball, and she wasn't ready to give it up just yet. The 2000 Summer Olympics were coming up in

Sydney, Australia. Hayley had a year to prepare for the softball training camp. She worked harder than ever to be competitive at both sports, while also studying full-time at Simon Fraser University in British Columbia. Her schedule was gruelling. She had softball practice in the mornings from 6:00 a.m. to 9:00 a.m. After practice, she was off to her science classes, keeping up a full university course load. Then, to keep her hockey skills sharp, she played with the University of British Columbia men's hockey team in the evenings.

HAYLEY'S ATHLETICISM STRETCHED FURTHER THAN HOCKEY. HERE SHE DIVES FOR A BALL AT A TEAM CANADA PRACTICE IN BRAMPTON, ONTARIO, JUNE 20, 2000.

Immediately after winning gold at the 2000 IIHF Women's World Championship in April, Hayley headed to the Canadian National Softball Team tryouts. She had trained hard, juggling the two sports she loved. Hayley might have been the last player chosen — but she was on the team! Hayley was proud of herself. She had made it because she had worked hard for it. Of course, being the last player chosen meant that she might not be a starter, but Hayley wanted to be a starter. Over the summer she worked tirelessly at her game. By the time the Sydney Olympics began that September, Hayley was a starting player, alternating between third base and left field.

Canada won only one game (defeating Italy 7–1) out of the seven they played at the Olympics, but their performance had been solid. Their games against Japan and New Zealand both went to an extra inning and they lost all but one game by a single run. Hayley had the highest batting average on the Canadian team, and a lot to be proud of. She also became the second Canadian woman to compete in both the Summer and Winter Olympics and the first woman to do so in team sports. To this day Hayley believes that making the softball team and starting in the Olympics is one of her biggest sports accomplishments.

LEGENDARY WINS

After the 2000 Summer Olympics, Hayley's life changed in some big ways. At the age of 22, she'd fulfilled her Olympic softball dream. Her experiences with the women's hockey teams had influenced her greatly — she took her responsibilities more seriously than ever. She had a new boyfriend who was the father of a baby boy, Noah. Hayley decided she needed to simplify things. Competing in two sports at the Olympic level and taking care of a baby was too much. One sport would be enough . . . so Hayley chose hockey. And with the 2002 Winter Olympics in Salt Lake City, USA, just around the corner, she needed to train.

HAYLEY OFTEN BROUGHT NOAH ON THE ICE TO SHARE IN THE TEAM'S VICTORY CELEBRATIONS.

DISASTER STRIKES

Hayley was named to the 2001 Canadian Women's National Team. The Women's World Championship would be held in April, in Minneapolis, Minnesota. But just before the tournament, Hayley injured the medial collateral ligament in her knee and could not play. The Canadian team prevailed, winning their seventh consecutive World Championship.

But would Hayley be off the injured list in time for the Olympics? She did extensive physical therapy and the careful work and patience paid off. Hayley had healed just in time for her to take part in the brutal training program developed by Canadian coach Danièle Sauvageau. Coach Sauvageau had the team work out at a Canadian Armed Forces base, using the army's obstacle course, cement walls and all. This team was going to be tough and ready. For extra practise, eight games were set up between Canada and the United States.

THE TEAM STUMBLES

Those eight games were dubbed the pre-Olympic tournament. On October 20, 2001, in Salt Lake City, Canada took to the ice with confidence. Veteran Cassie Campbell was the team captain, and Vicky Sunohara and Hayley were alternate captains. They felt the team was ready, but Canada lost that first game 4–1. It was early in the pre-Olympic season, so the team wasn't too worried.

They got on the plane and travelled to San Jose to play their second game, on October 23. They were pumped at the chance to even out the series, but at the end of the third period they headed to the dressing room with another 4–1 loss. Then the strangest thing happened to Hayley's team: they lost five more games in a row to the United States. Seven losses! What was happening?

Finally, on January 8, it was time for the last game in the pre-Olympic tournament. Canada had home ice at General Motors Place in Vancouver. Would the Canadian crowd see another devastating loss?

When the final buzzer sounded, the Canadian women filed to the dressing room with their heads hung. The score was a devastating 3–2 for the United States. They shut the door and the team sat silently for a while. Sweat dripped down Hayley's face. On the inside she was fuming. How could they have lost so many games? Something needed to change.

Finally, someone spoke up and said, "We played okay."

Hayley couldn't hold in her anger anymore. She stood up and said, "We lost eight in a row! This is not okay."

Suddenly, some players were shouting, others were crying and some were just sitting mute. Team Captains Cassie Campbell and Vicky Sunohara got the room under control. It was time to talk it out . . . so they did. When the team left the room hours later, things were different. They had discussed how they would work as a team both on and off the ice. They would play soccer together before games. They would eat together. They would motivate each other with slogans and cheers. They wouldn't listen to fans criticizing them. They would ignore the media and anyone else saying they couldn't do it. They would stick together. Nothing would get in the way of the belief that they could win the gold.

THE POWER OF BELIEF

GOING PRO

Team Canada's amazing performance in Salt Lake City fulfilled Hayley's Olympic hockey dreams. She had her gold. Now what?

Hayley wanted to get out of her comfort zone. Several hockey experts suggested that she try playing men's professional hockey overseas. The European leagues played a different, less physical, style of hockey. Hayley would have a shot at making a men's team there. This appealed to her, so she did some networking and signed with the Merano Eagles, in Italy's Elite A league, their highest level of hockey. But the day she went to pick up her travelling papers, she found out the Italian Ice Hockey Federation had just made a new rule: women were not allowed to play in the A league.

Hayley had been through not being wanted before, so she wasn't going to give up — she was going to find the right team. She turned down an offer with the Cincinnati Cyclones of the ECHL, and instead went to Finland for a 30-day tryout with the Salamat hockey club in Finland's second-highest league. They played out of Kirkkonummi, a town located just west of Helsinki. The team was coached by Matti Hagman, a former Edmonton Oiler. The day Hayley arrived,

Hagman took her aside and told her that she wasn't in North America anymore and no one was going to protect her on the ice. Hayley understood she wouldn't be getting any special treatment out there.

In her tryouts, the team's biggest defenceman followed Hayley everywhere. He dogged her on every drill. She worked hard to dodge him and play through. She had to prove that she could play in this league — and she did! Salamat offered Hayley a contract. The defenceman later apologized to Hayley. He said Coach Hagman had told him to shadow Hayley to prepare her to play against the biggest and toughest in the league.

The attention Hayley got for playing in the Finnish professional league was astounding. Whenever and wherever she played, fans and the media came to watch "the girl" play hockey. The attendance in arenas skyrocketed. Hayley didn't let her fans down. In her first game, she got a point on an assist. Hayley scored her first goal for Salamat on February 1, 2003, and went on to play 33 games with the team.

She is the first woman ever to score a goal in a men's professional league. In her first season with Salamat, she earned 11 points in 12 games and in the playoffs she tallied 7 points in 11 games. Salamat won the championship and was promoted to a higher division.

HAYLEY AND HER SALAMAT TEAMMATES CELEBRATE A GOAL.

Hayley went back to Finland for Salamat's 2003–04 season, but after playing 10 games she returned home. She missed her family, friends and especially her Canadian teammates. Plus, she was now a mother as well as a hockey player, and she wanted Noah to grow up in Canada alongside his grandparents and extended family. They moved back to Calgary, where Hayley signed with the Oval X-Treme women's team.

Hayley remains very proud of her professional league experience. Her success helped women in hockey gain respect in Canada and around the world.

BEST IN THE WORLD

Hayley was a talented veteran by the time she returned to Canada in 2003, but she still worked hard to improve. Before she knew it, it was time to play on another Olympic Team. The 2006 Winter Games in Turin, Italy would be her fourth — three Winter Games for hockey and one Summer Games for softball. Hayley was again selected as alternate captain for Team Canada and she couldn't wait to play.

The round-robin portion of the 2006 Olympics was a dream for the Canadian women. They won every game, with 36 goals for and only 1 against. Hayley had a five-point game against Italy, with a hat trick and two assists in their 16–0 victory. She then had a goal and two assists in Canada's 6–0 semifinal win against Finland. In a huge upset, Team USA had lost their semifinal to Sweden, which Canada would be facing off against for the gold.

At 3:15 into the final game, Gillian Apps, with an assist by Hayley, opened the scoring. By the end of the first period it was 2–0 for Canada. In the second period, the Swedish team played hard, but Hayley handily wheeled the puck around them, making a perfect pass to Cherie Piper, who tapped it in. Canada had a solid lead and didn't let up, winning the gold medal game 4–1. In a post-game interview, Hayley said, "The score may have made it look easy, but it definitely wasn't . . . It's definitely harder to defend gold than to win it."

It was a great Olympics for Hayley. She was the top scorer for the tournament, named both MVP and IIHF Best Forward and selected to the All-Star Team. In just five games she tallied an incredible 17 points, including 5 goals and 12 assists. Hayley was on top of the world.

HAYLEY WAS BORN AUGUST 12, 1978 . . .

. . . AND HER FAVOURITE COLOUR IS BLUE!

PRESSURE IS A PRIVILEGE

Hayley was busier than ever in the years following the 2006 Olympic win. Noah was a preschooler and Hayley juggled being a mom and taking university courses on top of keeping up the training regime of a top-level athlete.

During the 2008–09 season Hayley decided to play professional hockey once more. She brought Noah to Sweden with her where she played on

Linden HC, a men's team in the Swedish Division 1 league. Hayley played the better part of the season, but decided to return home early. Things were gearing up quickly for the 2010 Olympics and this time the pressure was immense. Canada was the 2010 host country and the world would be watching. The Canadian Women's National Team motto was "pressure is a privilege." Hayley and her teammates knew that defending a gold medal on home soil would be difficult. Canadian newspapers and television reporters talked endlessly about medals. There was a national campaign to win as many as possible. Canadians were counting on the women's hockey team to win gold — nothing else would do. Could the women defend their title again?

The Vancouver Olympics was huge pressure for Hayley — this time she was captain! She had captained the under-22 team for Canada in 1998, and she'd been an alternate captain for the Women's National Team since 2001, but to lead the Olympic Team in her home country was something else. Hayley knew she could do the job. Behind the scenes, the players tried to relax and enjoy the thought of so many of their friends and family coming to watch the games and cheer them on.

The tournament took place from February 13 to 25. Things started off on the right foot with Canada winning all three of their round-robin games, playing in front of huge crowds. During the game against Sweden on February 17, Hayley scored her second goal of the tournament and became the all-time women's leader in goals at the Olympics — a title she still holds today.

Canada was pitted against Finland in the semifinals. Hayley knew the Finns were serious about winning and she promised the media that the Canadians would not take them lightly. The Canadian women cruised to a 5–0 win in front of a crowd of 16,324. That was the most that many on the team had ever played in front of. The home country fans had been filling the seats at Canada Hockey Place to support their team.

All eyes were on the gold medal game, which took place on February 25 against their big rivals, Team USA. The arena was sold out, the cheers were deafening and the expectations were high. Before leading her team onto the ice, Hayley reminded them that this pressure was a privilege. After losing two Olympics in a row, the Americans would be hungry for a win.

In the first period, the Canadians were feeling that pressure, but goalie Shannon Szabados made some amazing saves with her impressive butterfly moves and glove work. Hayley and her team had found their groove. Young up-and-comer Marie-Philip Poulin scored twice and by the end of the first period the score was 2–0 for Canada. The game was a battle, with Canada getting six penalties in the first two periods. But veteran Hayley had perfected her penalty killing skills. She easily cleared the puck when the United States was on the attack and prevented them from scoring. After three periods of play, the US failed to get a single goal. Canada had won the gold medal! Captain Hayley wrapped the Canadian flag around her shoulders and skated around and around the ice, waving to the crowd. She'd had a great tournament, with two goals and nine assists for eleven points in five games.

CAPTAIN HAYLEY WICKENHEISER JUMPS ON GOALIE SHANNON SZABADOS AFTER BEATING THE US TEAM FOR THE GOLD AT THE 2010 OLYMPICS.

TIME TO QUIT?

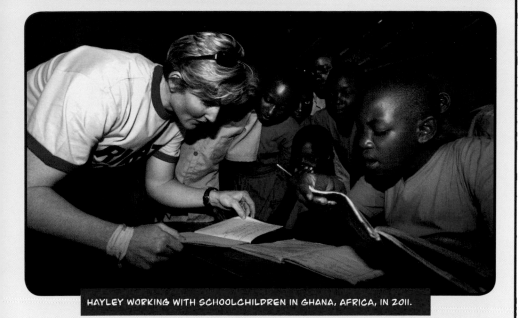

HAYLEY WORKING WITH SCHOOLCHILDREN IN GHANA, AFRICA, IN 2011.

After the 2010 gold medal performance, Hayley was practically a living legend. But even before she became a household name, she used her connections and time to share her love of sport with Canadians and people all over the world. In 2000, she became an athlete ambassador with the global organization now known as Right To Play, which uses the power of sports and games to help children who are facing adversity. On June 30, 2011, Hayley was coaching children in Ghana when she got a call from Canada. She had been named an officer of the Order of Canada by Governor General David Johnston. Hayley sent a press release from Ghana that said, "I want to thank all of you for your support. I'm very honoured to also receive the Order of Canada and thank organizations like Right To Play that have given me the chance to work with them."

THE HONOURS PILE UP

Shaunavon, Saskatchewan, is proud of their hockey hero. In 2011, a multi-million-dollar recreation centre opened there. It was named the Crescent Point Wickenheiser Centre. This was a big breakthrough for women's hockey and an honour that almost made Hayley speechless. During the opening-weekend festival, Shaunavon mayor Sharon Dickie spoke to the crowd. She said, "To Hayley: Welcome home and congratulations on your most recent award as a recipient of the Order of Canada, the highest honour a Canadian can hold. We have immortalized you forever in this community by proudly placing your name and your family's name on this facility and your museum within. I just want to say thank you for all that you have accomplished, and for being the strong role model and great Canadian that you are."

When Hayley got up to speak, she talked about raising awareness for community arenas in Canada. She also spoke to the kids, from her heart: "All of you kids sitting right here are going to have a chance to grow up in a new rink, and I can tell you that when I was your age, I never thought that I'd one day have my name on the side of a rink. It's really cool to be a female hockey player in Canada." That weekend was a proud celebration with family and friends.

ANOTHER OLYMPICS?

In June 2013, Hayley finally earned a bachelor of science degree in kinesiology from the University of Calgary. It had taken her much longer than the usual four years because of her hockey career, but Hayley had been determined to graduate — and she did.

Hayley could now focus on the task at hand: making the Canadian Olympic Team one more time. At the time of the 2014 Olympics in Sochi, Russia, Hayley would be 35 years old. She knew she could still play, having kept up her training. Hayley was strong and fit. But other people wondered if she was too old. Not everyone was convinced she could do it. Hayley had to prove herself all over again.

HAYLEY (MIDDLE ROW, CENTRE) AND THE 2014 GOLD MEDAL TEAM.

WICKFEST

The 2014 Olympics would be Hayley's last Olympic Games. She had proved to the world that she was still one of the best. She had competed in nine Women's World Hockey Championships, playing 41 games and earning 68 points; an astounding five Winter Olympics for hockey, playing 26 games, earning a total of 51 points and winning four Olympic gold medals and one silver; and competed in a Summer Olympics as a starting member of the softball team. Hayley had accomplished all she had ever wanted to on the international stage and decided to retire. But that didn't mean she was quitting hockey — not even close.

Hayley never forgot what it was like for her to improve her hockey skills when she was a girl. She remembered all those times she wasn't allowed to play. So in 2009 Hayley started a hockey school for girls, which today is called the Canadian Tire Wickenheiser International Female Hockey Festival, or WickFest. Once she retired, she had more time to focus on it, and WickFest grew like crazy. Girls come from across Canada and all over the world to learn how to skate better, pass, shoot, score, focus and seriously improve their game. Famous female players like Danielle Goyette, Natalie Spooner, Meghan Agosta and Shannon Szabados help run skills camps, and longtime friend Coach Wally Kozak is a key instructor. He teaches today's young players the same things he taught Hayley in her days on the Olympic Team.

Hayley has also continued to work with Right To Play, as well as with Jumpstart and KidSport, which are organizations that help kids with the financial costs of playing sports. She is widely respected, not just for hockey, but for her humanitarian work.

In January of 2018, she travelled to Leh, a remote village in the Himalayas and the home of hockey in India. On an outdoor rink, with the mountains in the background, Hayley taught skills to young women, an experience she believes for them was as much about empowerment as it was about learning how to play hockey.

But of all Hayley's many accomplishments, the one she is most proud of is seeing young girls walk into their local arena with their bags and sticks — and huge smiles on their faces.

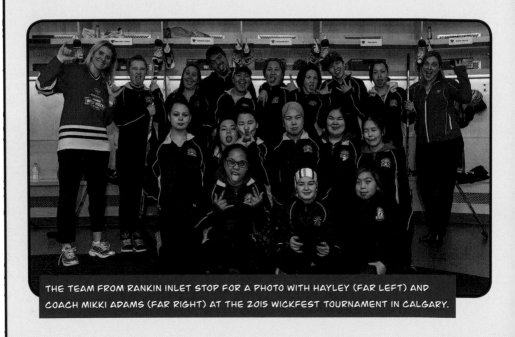

THE TEAM FROM RANKIN INLET STOP FOR A PHOTO WITH HAYLEY (FAR LEFT) AND COACH MIKKI ADAMS (FAR RIGHT) AT THE 2015 WICKFEST TOURNAMENT IN CALGARY.